TALES OF TERROR'S
SUBGENRES OF TERROR 2020
CLAUSTROCORE FILMS

SUBGENRES OF TERROR

2020 EDITION

STEVE HUTCHISON

CLAUSTRO CORE FILMS

FEATURING

STEVE HUTCHISON

CRITIC

First Printing: 2020
ISBN-13: 979-8616568939

Bookstores and wholesalers: Please contact books@terror.ca.

Tales of Terror
tales@terror.ca
www.terror.ca

INTRODUCTION

Included in this book are 50 reviews of horror and horror-adjacent claustrocore films.

Claustrocore films are about people stuck in one place for most of the running time.

Each book in the Subgenres of Terror 2020 collection contains a ranked thematic watchlist.

CONTENTS

BOOK OF SHADOWS: BLAIR WITCH 2
2000

6/8

Haunted tour participants awaken a supernatural entity while partying in the woods.

The Blair Witch Project; previous installment, relied on a gimmick so strong that the makers of Part 2 avoided it altogether. In fact, they often allude to it and make it an integral part of the plot but do not use it as a form of editing. Part 1 popularized the "found footage" genre by lying to its audience and was very good at it. Part 2 is more traditional but still worth a watch.

The actors are no longer playing pretend and improvising but their performances allow for great build-up despite sometimes obscured storytelling. Blair Witch 2 stirs up the same fear amalgams Blair Witch 1 did and proves that the original script doesn't only rely on opportunistic viral marketing. We get another terrifying mind-fuck depicting threats that cannot be taken down with weapons.

This is a well written and directed movie that didn't get the care it deserved in the cutting room. The compositing is excessive in places and comes out as more of a nuisance than a clever way to tell a scary tale. The layered narrative isn't needed. Some might hate this sequel as a complement to a game changer in the film industry, but as a stand-alone haunting story it hits all the right notes.

CLIMAX
2018

7/8

Dancers gather in a remote school to rehearse and party, unaware that the sangria is laced with LSD.

Give the movie a chance, if you're not into dancing, because surprises await. This is one of Gaspar Noé's most uplifting films, which doesn't mean he'll go easy on you. If you're familiar with the man, you know that he goes for the jugular. He still makes his camera glide, turn, flip, and do impossible things. His credit screens are still enigmatic, but there is method to his madness.

This must have required an unimaginable amount of preparation, rehearsal, and structure. Half the shots are long, interrupted sequences. At some point, you don't even notice it, which speaks volumes. The camera often travels from one character to another, telling many stories along the way. The actors are as talented with dialogue as they are dancing, which is a tour de force. Great casting!

Gaspar Noé is, as always, brutally honest. He takes us to a happy place and turns it into a living hell. See, what the protagonists don't know is that they've all ingested a heavy dose of LSD. They're slowly debilitating and there's no end in sight. You'll have to watch the movie to see just how far Noé takes his concept. Climax is both entertaining and traumatizing.

GRAVITY
2013

7/8

Two astronauts attempt to survive after their space shuttle gets destroyed, leaving them stranded in space.

Dialogue is precious, here, because there's not a lot of it and, when there is, the actors make every word count. Off-screen voices aside, there are only two characters, played by Sandra Bullock and George Clooney. This is one of the scariest movies ever made and it doesn't even use the tropes of horror cinema. Gravity is extremely agoraphobic. Sit tight!

The techniques used to achieve the illusion of weightlessness are puzzling and, at times, overwhelming. Metal rigs and special cameras were utilized. Most of the movie consists of CGI. You'll basically believe this film was shot in space. Be ready for over an hour of pure tension and touching moments whenever things slow down. Our hearts are, at all times, either pumping or shattering.

Expect breath-taking action scenes with mind-bending special effects that punctuate the story every so often. Audio design is extremely meticulous, seeing as there is no sound in space. It is not, at any point in time, clear what Sandra Bullock's character is trying to achieve, but it sure seems vital and very complicated... so much so that we lose hope, as she does.

127 HOURS
2010

7/8

A mountain climber becomes trapped under a boulder while exploring canyons alone.

This film is based on Aron Ralston's memoir Between a Rock and a Hard Place. Aron is played by James Franco. This could be called the performance of a lifetime, but that's all the man ever does. His character meets a virtually unsolvable problem that threatens his life, and we witness his delirium and desperation as the story progresses. Franco makes us cherish our lives, however miserable.

127 hours is about a young man with his arm stuck between a boulder and a wall. The question is: is this story sustainable as a feature film? Is there enough meat on this bone? Surprisingly, yes. After a short introduction, the inciting event traps the protagonist. His only escapes, until the end, are his memories, flashbacks and hallucinations. The film otherwise takes place in one location.

The editing is cool, extreme and imaginative. It's there to speed up things, transmit the weather or to convey emotions; mostly regrets. The protagonist comes up with many ways to solve his problem and must deal with a great amount of frustration when they fail. This film is also a confession; the admission of an overgrown ego and excessive self-confidence. 127 Hours is a brutal therapy.

BATTLE ROYALE
2000

7/8

The Japanese government secludes ninth-graders on a deserted island and forces them to kill each other.

Battle Royale's premise is ludicrous but memorable for the same reasons. It is a troubling drama interlaced with heartbreaking romance. At the core is an all-out war that can't end well. The film is tense from the first scenes in and foreshadows shocking events: students; friends and enemies, are forced to kill each other using randomly assigned weapons.

Two "wild cards" are thrown in the mix: a returning contestant and a psychopathic volunteer. They are battle-ready and they steal the show, casting a shadow on lesser characters. The weaker moments are highly philosophical and often anticlimactic, which might rub some viewers the wrong way. Fortunately, the action scenes compensate for the few weaker ones.

The island is gorgeous and filmed just right. It is made of beautiful plateaus, mountains and shores that would feel dreamy in a different film. The sadistic game's design makes good use of the environment and we get a good sense of geography. There are many characters for the script to manage so the pacing gets wobbly, but Battle Royale mostly keeps us biting our nails at the edge of our seats.

SAW 3D: THE FINAL CHAPTER
2010

7/8

The members of a dangerous cult turn against each other as they reach the last steps of their master plan.

We start with another clever contraption and this one is displayed on the public place, curiously. The tone is momentarily that of a cheap slasher, and then we're back to a more familiar tone. Hoffman, the bad guy, survived the last film and is now angrier than ever. He made mistakes, recently, and attempts to clean up any trace of the past leading back to him. It's starting to feel like the end.

Some survivor we don't remember is put through a new series of traps but only delays the last call. It's the feud between Jigsaw's widow and his disciple we care about and we do get closure. The tension is palpable, as always, and we even manage to sympathize for the villain who's always so purposely deliciously underplayed. The other actors do an excellent job and are an interesting bunch.

This is also a reunion of everybody not yet dead; from previous movies or by implication. This brilliant subplot sets the perfect context for a meaningful massacre. Well directed, written and shot, and when considering how many loose ends need tying, the seventh installment in the Saw franchise pulls miracles, with twists at every turn. Here's a great conclusion to a great horror epic!

SAW IV
2007

7/8

A detective has ninety minutes to solve a dangerous puzzle and save his colleague.

With Jigsaw now dead, we are left with a bunch of people trying to survive the games he left behind, manipulated by the thought of imminent death. How can the franchise survive the loss of its icon? That's what flashbacks are for. Because this was the intended direction, it comes as a strength more than a plot hole that requires patching. It allows us to cover clues left behind, for one thing.

Saw's typical narrative plays with perceptions of time and space to pull its crazy twists, yet, even at this point, they remain hard to predict. For the first time, we don't feel limited to one location. The cast is enlarging too. Aside from sporadic protagonist exposition, old characters return or get a backstory. This is one for the fans. It's filled with subtle references and Easter eggs.

We investigate Jigsaw's past and that of his followers and family; his relationship with his first victims and his wife in regards to his secret scheme, namely. Expect the same optimal quality and the excellent acting as the previous films, but a somewhat faster pacing. The transitions are stunningly creative in this one and use little CG. The same can be said about the traps and torture props.

SAW III
2006

7/8

Threatened by a deadly contraption, a doctor must perform brain surgery on her dying captor.

Two stories are being told at once. We follow both a surgeon who's forced to save the villain's life and a man stuck in an improvised labyrinth whose backstory is unclear. By now, we know we're in for gore and crazy twists. The two previous narrative structures were more intricately crafted, but this is by no mean a weak sequel. It certainly doesn't hold back.

The film's biggest weakness is that it pushes the creativity so far that it loses the shocking plausibility of the previous films. We're increasingly asked to suspend disbelief. The writing is still smart; just not its usual self. The horror, in this franchise, has been emanating from a clever, horrifying mix of dilemmas and schemes set up by an evil genius. This element is stronger than ever.

The torture devices are more aesthetic; not the ones that necessarily rip you apart. The editing is sometimes abusive, but then it also keeps things quick, with minimal dialogue and little filler. Continuity is remarkable. Even when considering the artistic liberties taken, this one is as homogeneous as the first sequel was; so much so that the series is slowly starting to feel like one big movie.

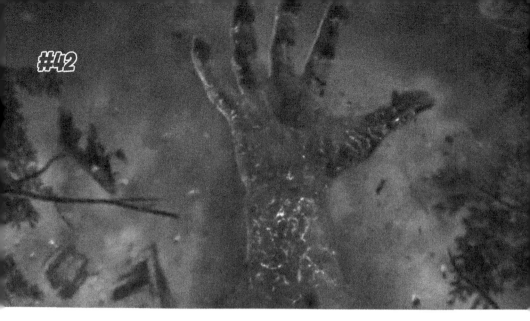

THE CABIN IN THE WOODS
2012

7/8

Five friends travel to a remote cabin where they get more than they bargained for.

The Cabin in the Woods is a parody of popular horror movies and horror movie tropes, including props, places and characters. Think of the desolated gas station, the mountain road, the remote cabin, the lake; all typically haunted by a killer with a mask and a weapon of choice. You get all the stereotypes, too; the dumb blonde, the jock, the scholar, the stoner and the virgin.

The casting isn't intuitive and character exposition, as extensive as it is, becomes futile because the Cabin the title refers to alters personalities. Clever! It's easy to spoil this film, considering the amount of twists it contains. The main thing you should know is that it was made for horror fans and, as such, it is a complete success. It is a surprise bag and it is unpredictable.

The creature design is well-done and, in some cases, very amusing. The creators manage to spoof big horror flicks while telling their own stories and, ultimately, without ruining the experience for the average movie-goer. Don't forget to blink, breath and hydrate yourself through the last act. It is an intense roller-coaster ride and it won't go easy on you!

THE HUMAN CENTIPEDE (FIRST SEQUENCE)
2009

7/8

A mad doctor kidnaps and stitches together three tourists from anus to mouth.

There are few things worse than a car breakdown leading you under a psychopath's scalpel blade. Getting stitched buttock to mouth to your best friend and to a stranger by the hand of a mad surgeon is one of them. Rarely has torture porn used such a strong gimmick. The synopsis alone inspires fear and disgust. The Human Centipede is downright traumatizing and may make you sick.

Aside from some frustratingly improbable subplots, and despite the surreal premise, you buy what you see on screen. It's well shot and not as cheesy as one might think. There is pretty much a single location and a small amount of well fleshed characters. This setup allows for confined build-up that culminates into an amazing claustrophobic carnage so intense some might feel like pausing the film.

You will not want to eat before, during or after watching, and it will mark you for weeks. The disgusting stuff is mostly implicit and the gore limited, yet we feel the pain. It builds tension masterfully, makes you fear the worst, gives you even worse than implied, mixes humiliation, kink, sadism, fetishism, even. It's one sick movie, but it hits all the notes the ideal horror movie should.

CRAWL
2019

7/8

A woman and her father find themselves trapped in a flooding house and must fight for their lives against alligators.

Michael and Shawn Rasmussen came up with a script that appeals to both creature feature and disaster film fans. By doing so, they avoid absolute clichés of both subgenres, which makes them unpredictable. The alligators are introduced very early on, which means that we get to know the main protagonist as she deals with danger, as she struggles, as she suffers.

The jump scares are epic. It's as if the alligators know they're in a horror movie. "Crawl" refers to the crawlspace Kaya Scodelario's character, Haley, is stuck in, with the water level rising, for most of the running time. It intensifies her situation and makes our hearts pump faster. Haley is a good swimmer, as we learn in the first scene, which will come in handy.

The storm is just as breath-taking as the alligator effects. You can't fake a condition like this one with practical effects alone, yet we don't feel the CGI. By the time the end credits roll, you'll believe alligators can take over your house. Crawl is an exciting ride, and it's better than most alligator horror films out there. The pacing is tight; the tension palpable. The actors are A1.

DEEP BLUE SEA
1999

7/8

A group of scientists on an isolated research facility are attacked by sharks.

Deep Blue Sea isn't Jaws. It gets up close and personal with the shark, instead, and most of the film takes place on an isolated aquatic search facility, which makes the movie confined and claustrophobic. You can always count on Renny Harlin, director extraordinaire, for turning a horror script into an action flick. Explosions, storm, floods; you get it all.

The facility's design is dope. Its conception is puzzling. It's pretty much a tridimensional maze. Passed the point of no return, it is in constant destruction, it burns from the inside and water runs through it. All hell breaks loose. These sharks are angry and vengeful. This isn't exactly a comedy, but some of the best parts are absolutely hilarious. The story is enthralling and very dynamic.

Thomas Jane is your typical American hero. He shoots first and asks questions later. Samuel L. Jackson plays the ass hole and gets the best lines. LL Cool J is the comic relief. He's fun and sympathetic. All things considered, Deep Blue Sea may very well be one of the best killer shark movies out there. It's unpredictable, action-packed, and it's larger than life.

DISTURBIA

2007

7/8

A teenager living under house arrest becomes convinced his neighbor is a serial killer.

Disturbia is reminiscent of Rear Window and Fright Night, but it's its own thing. The story is simple, and we've seen it countless time, but it was never told so lightly and with such an innocent tone. An interesting relationship evolves harmoniously between the three main protagonists. Two of them become romantically linked. The third wheel becomes the comic relief.

As a classic psychological thriller, the film hits every checkbox on the list. It's one of the best of its type. It is a quintessential thriller. It is intuitive. It flows admirably. It's predictable and, sometimes, predictable is fine. The performances are remarkable. Shia LaBeouf and David Morse are particularly good. Carrie-Anne Moss underplays.

Disturbia is brilliantly written and perfectly orchestrated to give us one hell of a ride. It has a lot of exposition, and that's not a problem. Part of the exposition involves a cute romantic arc that isn't realistic, very improbable, yet infinitely touching. Psychological thrillers are becoming a rarity but there is room for more and Disturbia proves it.

HARPOON

2019

7/8

Three friends find themselves stranded on a yacht in the middle of the ocean after a brutal argument.

The members of a conflicted love triangle end up stranded on a yacht in the middle of the ocean with a fishing pole, a harpoon, and not much else. What could go wrong? As it turns out, shit hits the fan pretty damn early, which leaves us about 60 minutes to deal with the consequences of the inciting incident. Harpoon has the blackest humor. Cancel your evening plans and watch it.

We learn a few things about Christopher Gray's character in the first act. He's jealous and possessive, he's violent, and he's an asshole. We know far less about his girlfriend, played by Emily Tyra, and their third wheel, played by Munro Chambers. There's an underlying mystery. There's a secret. Whatever it is, it's just the catalyst of a claustrocore nightmare.

You'll never want this film to end. Just when you think things couldn't get worse, it surpasses unthinkable thresholds. What it accomplishes best, every step of the way, is hit you with right hooks after a few jabs. You won't see it coming. Whatever you think you learn about these characters is only the tip of the iceberg. What great performances! And what a captivating story!

IDENTITY
2003

7/8

Stranded at a desolate motel during a rain-storm, a group of strangers start dying one by one.

Two things make Identity a marvel. First, it has one of the best twists in film history. You won't see it coming. Second, it has an incredible ensemble cast. We're talking John Cusack, Ray Liotta, Amanda Peet, John Hawkes, Alfred Molina, Clea DuVall, Jake Busey and Rebecca De Mornay. How can you go wrong with a team like that? How is this casting even possible?

The film is very dynamic, unpredictable, sporadically gory, tense, scary and a little bit sad. We go through a wide range of emotions in a short period of time. In a nutshell, it is inspired by Ten Little Indians. You can say this, of course, of every whodunit, but it's especially true here. Identity has a surreal aspect to it, and it doesn't exclude the possibility of a supernatural element.

Trying to guess who the killer is can be frustrating. The creators just won't give that away easily. Have fun guessing, but you'll probably fail. There are so many layers to Identity that it's worth watching over and over. Several clues are dropped and you'll probably miss them all. This is, simply put, one of the best psychological thrillers of its decade.

PONTYPOOL
2008

7/8

A radio host interprets the possible outbreak of a deadly virus contracted vocally.

Radio stations are such an atmospheric place to set horror movies. They're isolated, small spaces, and they require a limited cast. Radio hosts are often the first to learn about disasters and other incidents, and they warn the population about potential danger. Radio stations, ironically, are not protected from invasions by zombies and other contagious creatures.

We've got three talented leads. Stephen McHattie gives the most memorable performance as the news anchor. He has a witty sense of humor and gets the best lines. He's a little eccentric and somewhat self-centered. The relationship between him and his colleagues is particular. There's his ex and his assistant. We instantly buy their unusual chemistry.

The dialogue gets increasingly hypnotic, as the story unfolds. We're dealing with a disease that spreads vocally. That concept, in itself, is extremely imaginative. The fact that we absorb most of the explanation shows proficient writing. Our mind is constantly fucked with, but we always have an understanding of what the characters are going through. Lightning in a bottle!

DEAD END
2003

7/8

On Christmas Eve, on their way to a celebration, a family tries a shortcut and soon regrets it.

Dead End is as amusing as it is sinister. It's a Christmas-themed horror movie, but it couldn't be further from a celebration. It sends shivers down our spine on many occasions. It is suspenseful, it is sad, and it contains imaginative gore. The screenplay is clever and colorful. The film is told like a classic campfire tale. The budget is relatively small but that's never a problem.

Lin Shaye plays a mother who is losing grip on her family and, soon, on reality. Ray Wise is the abrupt and impatient husband and father, Mick Cain is the comic relief, Alexandra Holden the traumatized daughter and William Rosenfeld her boring boyfriend. These guys have great chemistry. We totally buy them as a family. When shit hits the fan, we sympathize instantly.

Most of the running time is spent inside and around a car, at night, and this probably wasn't easy to shoot. This movie being dialogue-driven, we're in good hands with writers and directors Jean-Baptiste Andrea and Fabrice Canepa. The actors deliver their lines effortlessly. It rolls off their tongues. The creators truly caught lightning in a bottle with Dead End.

THE MIST
2007

7/8

A mist unleashes bloodthirsty creatures on a small town, where a band of citizens hole up in a supermarket.

Frank Darabont, director and screenwriter, proves once again that he can adapt Stephen King's material like no one else. He can deliver, within budget, a stunning production quality. The actors are solid. The casting is excellent. Everybody fits their part. The action mainly takes place in one location; a grocery store, and the film is apparently shot on a sound stage. It's so claustrophobic!

The screenplay is ambitious. The creature design and most of the storyline could be described as Lovecraftian. The creatures' origin is and will remain a mystery. Their goal and motivations are never explained. As one of the character suggests, at some point, they are either supernatural, biblical or man-made. They could be anything. It's what makes them creepy. The mist itself is an enigma.

The 3D effects are a little too shiny for my taste, and that's the film's only flaw. As is often the case in apocalyptic movies, human's most resilient enemies are other humans. Religion and spirituality are crucial to the plot. Romance and family are important themes, too. The Mist is frightening, introspective, but it's also terribly sad. And what a great ending!

LIFE
2017

7/8

A team of scientists aboard the International Space Station discover a rapidly evolving Martian life form.

The first thing we notice about Life is its recreation of life in space, down to the last detail. No, this wasn't shot in weightlessness. It's one hell of an illusion. To emulate a lack of gravity, the actors were suspended by wires that wound up erased in post-production. The second thing we notice is the similarity with both 1979's Alien and 2013's Gravity.

You can compare this film to many, but, when all is said and done, it is its own thing. The creature design is simple but effective. The characters are not complex. Most are barely exposed. We care about them because we sure wouldn't want to be stuck in space with an alien creature that outsmarts us. This double threat creates a lot of anxiety. It's very claustrophobic.

The effects are ambitious and nearly perfect. The photography is so breath-taking you'll forget you're watching a movie. The acting is irreproachable. Some are big in Hollywood, some are unknown. All do a bang-up job. This is the kind of film that makes you think twice about space travel and alien life. As if it couldn't get cooler, Life is actually a slasher, of all things!

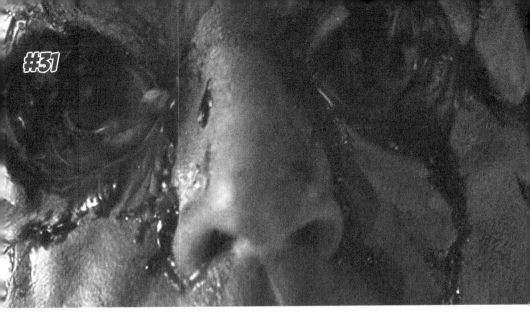

EVENT HORIZON
1997

7/8

A rescue crew investigates a spaceship that disappeared into a black hole and has now returned, severely altered.

You might agree, when all is said and done, that Event Horizon is everything horror science-fiction should be. It takes place in space, aboard a ship engineered by Sam Neill's character. Joely Richardson and Laurence Fishburne play important characters, too, and are friendlier. They will make you believe you're out there, with them, in space, about to be sucked into a black hole.

You wouldn't believe how much stuff is crammed into this film. It is relatively short and surprisingly dense, but it was heavily edited, as requested by the studio. It even has slow moments of calculated build-up. It always pays off. The script is clever, and the directing immersive. The costume design is appropriate, and a lot of thought went into the ship's design.

Of all things that can be said about Event Horizon, calling it Lovecraftian is no exaggeration. It is about the things that can't be described, unseen, forgotten, with a quintessential science-fiction procedural that drives us to the darkest corners of the mind. This is never mentioned with dialogue, but you can just feel it through and through. The deeper you get, the more you can feel it.

DON'T BREATHE
2016

7/8

Three thieves break into the house of a blind man who isn't as helpless as he seems.

In Don't Breathe, a handicap is only a weakness if it doesn't make you a badass. Stephen Lang plays a war veteran who's simply defending his home and fortune against three bums. As it turns out, the thieves are the protagonists, and they're in big trouble. Silence is powerful, here. The man whose property they are trespassing on is blind, but quite resourceful.

Like him, the camera is highly dynamic, ominous and omnipresent. The editing is impeccable, and particularly when it comes to audio. The script is tight, despite the small story. Don't Breathe is a claustrocore film with no fluff, no filler, and, despite a slow pacing, no second is wasted on trivial plot details. As surreal as it appears, the film is strangely plausible.

Jane Levy and Dylan Minnette's characters easily outlive Daniel Zovatto's, who was predestined to die, with his shitty attitude and his lack of depth. Also, this movie, passed the halfway mark, introduces a key element that makes us reconsider everything we've seen; something so horrible that our attention gets shifted and everything we took for granted gets deconstructed and shuffled.

THE HOLE
2001

7/8

Four teenagers uncover and explore the depths of a sealed underground bomb shelter.

The Hole is at times poignant, frustrating, disturbing, but there is more, here, than meets the eye. This is a legendary mindfuck. The story is simple enough, but it gets increasingly layered the deeper we get. Parallel to the main timeline is a psychiatric investigation. This leads to one of the most powerful twists in the history of horror films and it happens sooner than you'd think.

Things gets very sinister passed a certain point. The teenagers realize they are locked inside the bunker they were partying in. Claustrophobia ensues. All this happens while the main protagonist, played by Thora Birch shows her unrequited love for Mike, one of two jocks, played by Desmond Harrington. Keira Knightley plays the hot chick and Laurence Fox her fling. All four are exceptional!

We get a good understanding of who everybody is, and they all react appropriately through the obstacles ahead. They are not exactly stereotypes; they remind us of people we know. They remind us of us. This film has a great kick, but it particularly stands out because of how shocking it gets. The suspenseful score makes everything better, and what an immersive bomb shelter set!

CABIN FEVER
2002

7/8

Isolated in a cabin in the woods, a group of friends become infected by a fast spreading disease.

If Cabin Fever at first behaves like any horror movie taking place in a remote cottage, it in fact finds its identity in that the main threat is an infectious disease. It starts simply enough with friends, including couples, seemingly supportive of each other but, then, traitors to each other when in jeopardy. The actors do a fine job with a vacillating script and sometimes odd dialogue.

The humor, here, is somewhat derived of inside jokes that we don't always fully get. It's a style, but it's consequently amateurish in its presentation. Paranoia, isolation and contagion are the fears the film plays on, and it's excellent at it. Between what you see, what is suggested and what you imagine, gore reminds you that this isn't just a psychological thriller.

The disease spreads so fast that it is played for a cringe and a laugh. By its raging scope, the plague is depicted as some impersonal slasher icon, with proper pacing, structure and body count. The sets, the score and the photo are reminiscent of similar subgenres, but, under this lens, the material is fresh enough on its own to generate something unique, entertaining, funny and sinister.

PUPPET MASTER: THE LITTLEST REICH
2018

7/8
Puppets gathered for auction at a convention are magically animated and kill everyone.

Puppet Master: The Littlest Reich is very loyal and respectful of the Puppet Master franchise but does things better and differently. It reinvents itself in every way possible while upholding most of the mythos. Something needed to be done because this series was going nowhere interesting. This new addition doesn't conflict with previous films and feels like both a sequel and a remake.

Continuity is maximized and there are no plot holes, except perhaps Andre Toulon's arc, which doesn't make a lot of sense. The whole Nazi versus Jewish element is kind of heavy, but it's been hindering these movies since the beginning and it must exist. The Littlest Reich has, by far, the best puppetry we've seen. The actors are excellent, no matter how significant their part is.

This mostly takes place in a hotel. It is where it all started, after all, and Puppet Master purists will appreciate it. The best thing about this movie is that the puppets are evil, so expect a slasher and a significant body count. There are boobs and there is sex, in case you wondered. The creators left nothing to chance. In fact, this may very well be the best Puppet Master movie to date.

MONKEY SHINES
1988

7/8
A quadriplegic man's trained monkey becomes psychotic.

The best stories are the simple ones. They're the ones easily described. They can be summed up in one sentence. This one is about a quadriplegic man and an evil monkey. One thing that makes Monkey Shines fascinating is the mental state the protagonist is in. He's suicidal. He's angry. He's not a plain victim. And the monkey, his tormenter, is entertaining, to say the least.

This is a slow-burn. Things take a while to pick-up. There is a ton of character exposition. Obviously, we can't have a monkey killing a bunch of people for over an hour and a half. This must have been a difficult shoot. Having the monkey do what it does was probably no easy task. This was George A. Romero's first studio film and he didn't exactly appreciate his experience.

Monkey Shines is one of the best horror movies about an animal gone mad. It's sad, surprising, it's well done, it's unpredictable and it has a good twist. Jason Beghe, the main actor, does a lot with the limited use of his body and while interacting with a trained animal. There is real proximity between us and the characters. The sequence of events is plausible and possibly a tad supernatural.

OLDBOY
2013

7/8
A man imprisoned for twenty years then set free seeks answers and revenge.

The original Oldboy was a product of South Korea that didn't get the international credit it deserved, probably because of subtitles and the cultural barrier. Additionally, it was presumably considered too surreal and convoluted for a mainstream audience with a generally lower attention span. That said, the emotions stirred up by this masterpiece are universally compelling and relatable.

This is a tale of sadness, remorse and frustration disguised as a revenge story that doesn't exactly following the tropes of the subgenre. It is far from predictable but is filled with plot holes that it dares blame on surrealism. The film's biggest flaw is that its story progresses as we witness events the protagonists aren't aware of, yet they pickup on the invisible clues left for us.

We get the cream of actors and equivalent deliveries. The photography and the effects are impeccable. The eccentricities that created a buzz about the 2003 version are brought back and treated with respect, skill and innovation. Every technical challenge is reattempted and revised, then upped a notch. This film will make you face taboos in ways you can't imagine, unless you've seen the original...

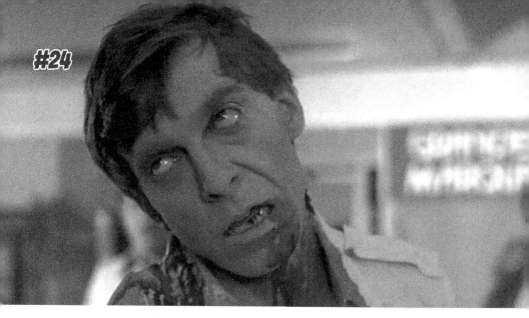

DAWN OF THE DEAD
1978

7/8

A zombie outbreak forces different professionals to remain barricaded inside an empty shopping mall.

George A. Romero's Night of the Living Dead, released in 1968, introduced a new creature to horror movie fans. It was neither a demon nor a vampire. It behaved somewhat like the Haitian zombie, but with a trigger event that was viral rather than Vodou. Dawn of the dead celebrates the new decade by upgrading his living dead. They're more coordinated, funnier, fun...

The ensemble cast is part journalists, part SWAT officers, so we get both warm and cold perspectives on the situation. The make-up is horrendous, the zombie acting fake, but the ambiance is breath taking. Most of this sequel takes place in a large empty mall that they try to infiltrate. As frantic as this film gets during its key scenes, it is generally slow paced. What's more, it's now in color!

Black and white made the original creepier, so Romero used color as a tool, here, using it to his advantage, and innovated. This is a comedy, something Night of the Living Dead wasn't. The characters are contrasted, the gore is bright and purposely fake, and there is credible physical contact during the many action scenes. Many bullets are shot and more zombies die than you can possibly imagine!

CUBE ZERO
2004

7/8
A prison operator infiltrates the rigged labyrinth he controls to save a victim.

The little backstory and the few answers Cube 2: Hypercube provided led us to believe humans; possibly government officers, were nothing more than suited scientists of the future doing cervical experiments. Some might have felt Part 2 revealed too much and undershot the enigma. Cube: Zero, presumably a prequel, takes place in the rusty rooms and around the traps of a three-dimensional prototype.

What's more, evil is given at least four faces. Two of them are compelling protagonists who set a fun tongue-in-cheek tone. They are the better part of the backstory we get; other bits going as far as imaging life outside the cube that should have ended up on the cutting room floor. We are fed too much detail about the fact this this one takes place in the future and in our world.

We care little for the people inside the maze since we already know how their story goes and ends. Zachary Bennett plays Eric, the most interesting and strongest character in the franchise. He is who we worry about. His arc is immense and his perspective on the mystery makes him the perfect protagonist of a smart, well-written sequel. Part 1 was great, Part 2 was good and Part 0 is a blast!

CUBE
1997

7/8
Amnesic strangers awaken in a three-dimensional booby-trapped maze.

Imagine an existential slasher where the murderers are the booby-trapped cubic rooms of a futuristic and potentially alien three-dimensional labyrinth. This larger than life horror take on Rubik's cube works miracles with limited but brilliant production design that takes us out of our element and into a world of technology, traps, math, doubt, repetition, confusion and fear.

Much like its architecture, this science-fiction slasher feels like a game; like a puzzle. As such, it encourages its victim to think more than act if they want to survive. The different cubic rooms are trapped in imaginative ways to generate striking gore. The characters are amnesic and start in the cube. There is therefore little to no character exposition aside what pertains to the plot.

Cube is close to flawless. Considering its small budget, much like its heroes, the makers used their brain to come up with a gimmick that create both an illusion and a nameless subgenre that translates to "puzzle horror". Only one room was used to shoot the whole maze. The illusion is seamless! This is a mystery, so expect more questions than answers. It's part of the game...

KRAMPUS

2015

7/8

A boy accidentally summons a demon before Christmas.

When it comes to Christmas horror, Krampus is as good as it gets. It starts as a tongue-in-cheek comedy poking fun at everything bad there is about the holidays, from kids fighting constantly to the bad side of the family, and joking avidly about capitalism, bad food, and even religion. As the story unfolds, we discover the more dramatic side of a script that only gets better with time.

The exposition is priceless. The best actors are given more prominent roles. We're talking Adam Scott, Toni Collette, David Koechner and Emjay Anthony, who all show a wide range of emotions. The most interesting aspect of Krampus is its supernatural element. It is extremely imaginative. The creature design is exactly what a child's mind would come up with, so why has no one attempted this before?

Snow, wreaths, colorful lights, holiday music, candles, presents, a Christmas tree; you get it all. Add to that a bunch of despicable characters who've probably been naughty all year long, and the "shadow of Santa Claus", and you're in for a horrific experience. The writers are not afraid to be politically incorrect and it pays off. Watch out for that second half; it's out of this world!

SAW II
2005

7/8

A SWAT team leader negotiates with a terminally ill murderer in attempt to save his son from a poison and a booby-trapped maze.

Jigsaw, the contraption serial killer, gathered a bunch of people in a condemned building and puts them to the test, again; this time as a group. Pushed to their limits, all characters eventually become hostile to each other. This is, in a way, Saw on a larger scale. The pace is faster, the cast larger, and the game more complex.

The story blends well with the first movie, some characters return and there is stunning continuity. The visual style and the filtered photo match the original picture. No plot detail is left to chance and every subplot finds its purpose. Expect the same score, excellent performances, significant production quality, the same frantic editing, and, of course, high shock and stress value.

Half of it takes place in Jigsaw's workshop, with a villain on the verge of death and with nothing to lose: someone that can't be threatened or reasoned with. He watches people die one by one in the most creative ways, something we now expect from the creators. The gimmick is simple: suffer or die suffering. It's not much of a choice, but it's terrifyingly relatable and horribly satisfying...

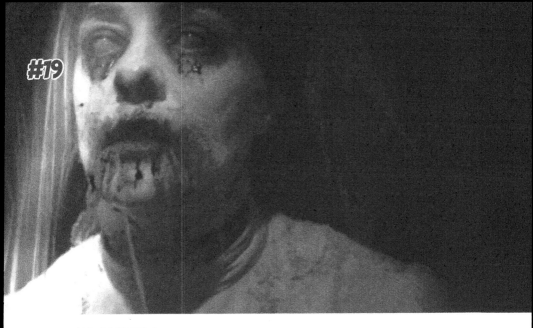

THE INNKEEPERS
2011

7/8

Two employees determined to reveal a hotel's haunted past experience disturbing events.

Watch the cutest, loveliest and most adorable pixie get bored for over 90 minutes when she should be seriously worried about her future. This is probably not going to end well for her. She is funny, fascinating and is extremely expressive, which allows her to carry most of the film on her shoulders. You'll hopefully fall in love with her. Ti West, writer and director, really wants you to.

There is wonderful chemistry between Sara Paxton and Pat Healy, which reflects on their respective characters. The strongest aspect of The Innkeepers is the exposition. The goal isn't as strong as the journey, so enjoy every second! This film was obviously inspired by Stanley Kubrick's The Shining. It is sprinkled with jump scares you won't soon forget.

Ti West's specialty is to let us simmer and never boil. Suspense in injected in small doses and the horror is close to inexistent, yet we expect it at every corner. Don't worry, by the time the end credit rolls, you'll be filled with terror and shivering. This is an unconventional ghost story and an excellent one. It is one of Ti West's best movies.

HOUSE OF WAX
2005

7/8

A group of teens stranded in a village near a strange wax museum realize their lives are in danger.

Elisha Cuthbert, Jared Padalecki, Paris Hilton, and Chad Michael Murray make this film epic, though it would still impress without them. They're not just talented actors, they remind us of people we know. They make this film fun and comfortable before it gets increasingly dark. This is the second time this story gets remade, and it is quite an enhancement. It's a slasher with an edge.

The writers know what a good movie is and that's exactly what they're giving us. They bank on common horror tropes, half the time, and somewhat re-invent them otherwise. The antagonists follow the same logic. We've seen their patterns before, but never quite like this. The budget is substantial, and the movie needs it to tell a big story. The set decoration and the special effects are massive.

Some of the pain inflicted is atrocious and, at times, hard to watch. The gore is brilliant. In regard to who bites the dust and in which order, the script does a pretty good job of keeping us guessing and on the edge of our seat. Personality flaws end up being assets. People we thought were protected by the writers get mutilated. You just can't take anything for granted. Great flick!

THE PEOPLE UNDER THE STAIRS
1991

7/8

Three burglar break into a house occupied by a dangerous couple and become trapped.

This film works like a charm for the same reasons Goonies did, except that it's made for an adult audience despite the main protagonist being a kid. The kid is basically stuck within the walls of a giant house owned by psychos. This is written and directed by Wes Craven. It's one of his most accessible films and is easily overlooked. It's right up there, in the upper tier of his filmography.

There isn't really something bad to say about this picture. It's in its own category. The special effects are strong. The cinematography is outstanding, considering some characters move between the walls. This must have been amusing but challenging to shoot. The actors are excellent and the characters they play are colorful. The villains, especially, are bigger than life.

The People Under the Stairs is atmospheric, tense, exciting, never boring; it is paced intelligently, it's a crescendo of terror and it's a damn good horror thriller. The title of the film can be misguiding. There are several layers to this story that make it stand out; that make it unique. In a sea of horror movies, this is the kind of stuff fans tend to come back to. It's rewatchable. It's fun.

NIGHT OF THE DEMONS 2
1994

7/8

Teenagers unknowingly carry a demon curse from a haunted house to their school on Halloween night.

1988's Night of the Demons was self-contained. Against all odds, Joe Augustyn performs a tour de force, here; powerful enough to bring back all the elements that made the original a classic, and carries the action from the haunted house to a Catholic boarding school; the second next best context for sexually frustrated teenagers. This is pretext, of course, for brattiness and blood...

The only thing the original had that the sequel doesn't is script purity. The arc was simple, and so were the characters. The writing is more layered in Part 2 and not as lively, but continuity is ensured by creative minds. As a sequel, it succeeds in further exposing the virulence of its creature with little redundancy: they are re-established as sexual demons that rely on fluids to possess.

Aside from centering on religion and the occult, the film meets every standard set by the original: deliberately bad but not terrible actors, imaginative practical effects, shock value, teen hormones and a lot of partying. Night of the Demons 2, like its predecessor, is more entertaining than intellectual, more humorous than dramatic, but manages to mix comedy and horror in 80's retro fashion.

NIGHT OF THE DEMONS
1988

7/8

On Halloween night, partying teenagers stir up spirits inside an abandoned house after a seance.

Like all marketable horror films of the 80's, Night of the Demons is an inexhaustible source of cheese, gore and partial nudity, has a strong gimmick and a catchy sonata. Few movies summarize quintessential b-horror like this one, though. It combines tropes of many major subgenres, namely haunting, possession, slasher and witchcraft. By genre tradition, it features teenagers in their 20's, too.

Several aspects of the film make it one of the best horror productions out there. Contrary to vampires, zombies and werewolves, demons are an ill-defined antagonist in horror movies. In Night of the Demon's case, they are as vocal, magical and virulent as Evil Dead's and as physically threatening as 1985's Demons'. In all three instances, the invasion is limited to a confined location.

The dialogue is disorganized and the acting exaggerated, yet the end product is so unique that it might as well be considered a deliberate directorial decision. The characters are dumb. The subplots are silly when not downright hilarious. The ambiance is highly pertinent for a Halloween setup and the style is so cohesive that Night of the Demon's cursed "land" comes out as a suspension of reality.

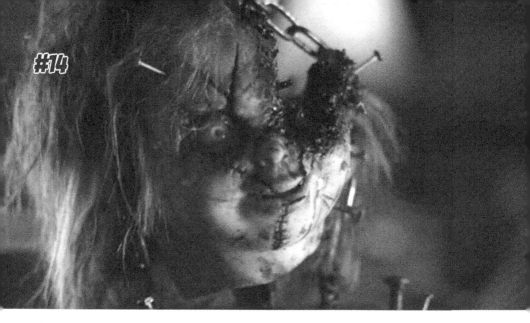

CULT OF CHUCKY
2017

7/8
A possessed doll infiltrates a psychiatric hospital.

After you've gone through an opening so nerve-racking you just might swallow your tongue, you're transported to a sanitarium, of all places, where all the good stuff is about to take place. Like Curse of Chucky, this film centers on Fiona Dourif's character; Chucky's daughter, who's about the furthest thing there is from a stereotypical final girl.

Cult of Chucky is a fascinating mindfuck with more twists and turns than any of its predecessors. You won't see most surprises coming until they hit you right in the face. The murders are gory and look cool as hell. The photography surpasses all we've seen up to now. Chucky never looked so good and so alive. We can no longer tell how he is animated from shot to shot.

Don Mancini, writer, director and franchise owner, learned a lot from "Curse", the previous film. The last thing he wants is another Seed of Chucky. He follows Curse of Chucky's winning combination to a T: put the scares and the mystery first; the humor and the Easter eggs second. That being said, all Chucky movies should be watched in order. They are first and foremost made for fans.

THE FINAL GIRLS
2015

7/8
Four friends get pulled into a 1980s slasher and must avoid getting killed.

This slapstick comedy isn't afraid to get dramatic to get its point across, but 95% of it is delirious. It is fascinating and hysterical. It's a spoof of Friday the 13th, first and foremost, but it's also about a cyclic time loop, it's meta, and it's an unusual time travel movie. It's also claustrocore in its own way. Every second of this gem is fascinating and unprecedented.

The characters are a likable bunch, even the ones in the film within the film. They get our imaginations running wild. Adam Devine and Angela Trimbur are hilarious as the two dumbest 80's slasher flick stereotypes a writer could possibly come up with. The way the two realities merge is far-fetched, but it's better to roll with it, considering where the script takes us if we suspend our disbelief.

Billy Murphy's design is as close as possible to Jason Voorhees', and it's impressive how much the creators got away with. In this film, the killer comes second. The Final Girls is all about the survivors. This production nears perfection. The dialogue is right out of a stand-up comedian's mouth. Everything in the script feels calculated. This is an ode to horror movie fans.

CURSE OF CHUCKY
2013

7/8

A woman whose mother recently died suspects a mysterious doll might be responsible and a hazard to her niece.

We start with the assumption that the audience knows Chucky. The best thing about this one is that it embraces its root; a time when tongue in cheek horror was praised. Chucky used to be scary, but then got turned into a joke. Well, he thankfully inspires fear again. One of the main protagonists is a kid and we rediscover the evil doll again through a plot reminiscent of the original Child's Play.

The image is clean and crisp. The cinematography is studied and calculated, and many shots are set up in a complex fashion. The story manages to be both amusing and serious; at the same time and in alternation. The score is at time psychedelic, especially in moments of tension which the film excels at. Brad Dourif, the voice of Chucky, returns. The rest of the cast is motivated and performs well.

The main set is a beautiful mansion and the action mainly takes place on a rainy night. Along with a script that gives you all you wish for, the cutting-edge effects, animatronics included, return with a new upgraded but faithful look. The film's weaknesses can easily be overlooked, seeing how many surprises await you. Also, this new addition to the franchise has more than one twist in store...

THE OTHERS
2001

8/8

The mother of two photosensitive children becomes convinced that her house is haunted.

This is the kind of film you want to watch in one streak, without interruption and in the right mood, because subsequent viewing won't be as impactful. A lot of this production resides in its surprises, scattered here and there, and in its twists. The Others will definitely become your go-to movie about ghosts for its quintessence and its haunting atmosphere.

Nicole Kidman deserves praise for her acting. She's not playing your run-of-the-mill mother. First, this is a period piece. Second, she's isolated in the middle of nowhere. Third, her husband is at war. Fourth, her kids are weird. There is more to this character than meets the eye. We know this because the first shot of the movie presents her in a state of panic. Her character never gets better.

Every word, in The Others, has a meaning. Alejandro Amenábar, writer, director and musician, shows you what he thinks you should see. His film is slow but surprisingly dense. The cast and sets are limited, but the film looks like a million bucks. It is visually rich, it is immersive and it's scary as hell. Also, all the actors, even the young ones, do a bang-up job.

**#10**

THE THING
1982

8/8

In Antarctica, a group of scientists comes in contact with a hostile alien parasite that lurks inside their camp.

This is a remake of the movie The Thing from Another World, a 1951 John W. Campbell story adaptation. The actors are all male and all geared up to face the worst conditions; more specifically, here, an upcoming battle against a powerful being that wraps itself in mystery. The "Thing" can hardly be summarized with words and doesn't communicate the way we do.

The Thing establishes suspense like few horror films do; by laying down the facts, raising questions that may never find answers, then offering you so much more than the many outcomes you could possibly imagine. It uses perfectly paced sequences leading to unexpected jump scares. The animatronics are one of the kind and among the best and scariest ever seen in the genre.

The lighting is always just right; not revealing too much or too little. The thick ambiance is reinforced by an ongoing storm that implicitly restricts and locks the protagonists in; therefore accommodating the creature and forcing the victims to find creative ways to survive. Fortunately, they have big muscles, free access to a large arsenal and aren't the scared type...

1408
2007

8/8
A man is trapped inside a hotel room and terrorized by ghosts.

At its purest form, 1408 is a condensed version of The Shining. This is obvious. The film is based on a short story by Stephen King and he can rip off his own material if he feels like it, but is it worth watching? 1408 needs to be considered a stand alone film and appreciated as such. It contains enough fresh material and twists you won't see coming. All in all, this is a great movie. Here's why...

First, it stars John Cusack in one of the best roles of his glorious career. Samuel L. Jackson is there to shuffle the deck. He wants to help, he's friendly, yet he's ominous. This is one of the most claustrophobic horror movies ever made. It's basically about a man stuck in a hotel room from another dimension. He should be surrounded by people and traffic, yet he couldn't be more isolated.

The acting is irreproachable. The limited set and cast are an advantage. Horror is mostly psychological, here, and it will send shivers down your spine on many occasions. One of 1408's creepiest cards is making your imagination wander. Exactly how far does room 1408's reach extends? At what point, in the film, does the haunting start? The more you think, the scarier this film gets...

EVIL DEAD
2013

8/8

Tricked into a week-end of rehab in a remote cabin by her friends, a girl in withdrawal believes she is surrounded by demons.

Technically second remake of a 1981 revolutionary cult classic, this movie has one of the strongest horror fan bases in history and a new generation of teenagers to seduce. The purists might bump on a few details, but none of the franchise's gimmicks have been overlooked and the movie looks like a million bucks. The gore effects are incredibly realistic and are torture even to the audience.

Bruce Campbell's Ash isn't part of the story, but his design and wit are found across the production. The performances range from forgettable to awesome, and it seems to be what the producers were after. This was also true of all previous films. Some actors hold back because the script wants them to until they get their special moment, at which point they unleash their true talent.

From photography to the narrative, every aspect of Evil Dead is calculated. It knows how to scare, disgust and make you jump, and does so with perfect timing. Humor is limited, much like the original Evil Dead. The biggest shift in tone between this and the first two is in the polish and the technology at hand. Nothing is left to chance. Expect twists and Easter eggs from beginning to end.

SAW
2004

8/8

Chained to pipes in a disused bathroom, two men are given a puzzle to which they must provide answers.

Saw is both a torture film and a police procedural. It's a ongoing mystery that explores new grounds in storytelling. It's refreshing and unique, yet closely reminiscent of the Cube franchise and Se7en. The power of this movie resides in how it cleverly parses clues, how complex the puzzle is, and how twists and turns reveal themselves. They do so in the most creatively shocking fashion.

The writing is brilliant. The photography is impeccable. Extreme color balance, photo filters and quick editing gives this movie a particular trademark. The actors do a fine job of keeping us guessing, sympathizing, cringing. Their performances make you feel as powerless as their characters become. One of the two main plot lines happens in one place and with only two characters.

While the cast is limited, each of their movements, lines and performances has been scrutinized and polished. When dialogue makes room for gore, Saw shows another significant strength; displaying pain and suffering crudely and realistically, thanks to stunning top-of-the line effects. Innovative, yet formulaic, Saw gives us a new horror icon with its own sonata; a nod to slasher flicks.

ALIEN
1979

8/8

An ore harvesting crew discovers a dead alien and large unidentified eggs inside an abandoned spaceship.

From stasis cages and poorly lit tunnels to the deep isolation of space, and considering how small the sets appear to be, Alien is vividly claustrophobic. It succeeds both on the horror and science-fiction levels. It's disorienting from the start and confinement isn't even the horror of it all. There is a giant extra-terrestrial aboard the ship and it's more a monster than a cute humanoid.

The beast is gradually revealed but never fully. Mystery and build-up are some of the many strengths of the well-paced script. There is unifying rigor in the creature and ship design. The rooms aren't just atmospheric; they are conveniently built, from the storyboard phase, to inspire distress. In a way, after all, this is a slasher taking place in space with, for victims, bored public workers.

The cinematography is a delight; always mastered, always vibrant. The effects are something else. If you needed a reason to fear alien invasion, this is it. They are depicted as smart but too savage, too animalistic to negotiate. Dense in detail and scientific procedural, Alien is high caliber sci-fi that's virtually flawless on all aspects and speaks to a rather intellectual niche.

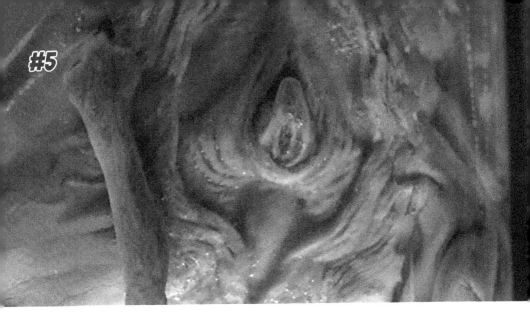

ALIENS
1986

8/8

The survivor of a space invasion awakened from stasis by her employer is asked to assist a troop of soldiers in hunting aliens.

Ripley, played by returning actress Sigourney Weaver, is offered a promotion if she resumes her nightmare. She accepts, curiously, but for the good of a franchise's birth. This time, her friends have big guns! They are not pencil pushers stuck in space; they're tough soldiers on a kamikaze mission. Aliens is more military and borrows from action flicks, as well as horror and science-fiction.

Everything is bigger, more frantic, rougher. There is sporadically elongated group dialogue and the movie has many crowded, elaborate battle scenes. It also behaves like a slasher film, as the support characters meet their end in dark corners. There is plenty of room for character exposition and it significantly pays off when things get tense and out of control as the bodies start piling up.

The players are vivid, cartoonish, superficial but purposely and not more than your average video game character. The effects range from rear projection to puppetry; all taken to gigantic proportions, this time. The detailed sets match those of the original. Elements that were left unexplored the first time around are given a meaning and a purpose. This certainly lives up to the original!

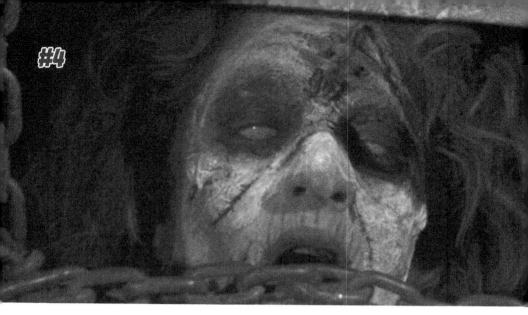

THE EVIL DEAD
1981

8/8

Teenagers partying in a cabin in the woods become possessed by demons.

The Evil Dead is everything a horror movie fan can wish for. It is also the ideal place to start for the uninitiated. Contrary to most films of its genre, it never relies on filler and barely exposes its protagonists. It makes its way to the trigger event quickly and soon plunges the story into somewhat of an extended third act. It's frightening, engaging, it's a little bit funny and very gory.

Some camera shots used have never been seen before and rely on creative rigs that director and writer Sam Raimi pulled out of a hat. His magic doesn't stop there. He gathered the right crew to produce a combination of claymation, latex, animal viscera and make-up that looks nothing like other films of the early decade. This is a good example of accessible experimental cinema.

Take The Exorcist, inject a generous dose of franticness, crank the violence to a maximum, get rid of the dialogue and you get this superficial gem! The Evil Dead is flawed when it comes to special effects, but they involve such unique cinematographic innovations that they are genuinely disorienting and terrifying, regardless. It is the quintessential horror movie and one of the best ever made.

MISERY
1990

8/8
An injured author is held captive by a deranged fan of his.

Here's the ultimate 1990's thriller. It is so intense that it can also be considered one of the best horror movies ever made. It is based on a novel by Stephen King; what more can you wish for? Small characters aside, this is a condensed emotional duel between Kathy Bates and James Caan. Misery is the perfect storm: perfect cast, perfect novel, perfect script and one hell of a director!

Bates plays a dangerous nut job and Caan the vulnerable victim; the writer she's a die hard fan of. If genders were inverted, these would be stereotypes. King explores a writer's nightmares, as he often does, but this is one of his greatest works. The film is sad, violent and extremely stressful. Some scenes will make you hold your breath and keep you on the edge of your seat.

Every subplot is executed with calculated timing. Nothing feels superfluous and there are no slow moments. The film is somewhat slow-paced but something horrible is at all times developing or getting out of control. This is one of the best Stephen King adaptations out there. Misery is, quite simply, nothing less than a perfect film. You need to see this... now!

GREMLINS 2: THE NEW BATCH
1990

8/8

An innocent allergic creature gives birth to a hoard of morphing monsters inside a commercial skyscraper after being exposed to water.

Gremlins 2 starts with a short Bugs Bunny gag as if to establish it is now a perked version of itself. It's slightly more suitable to a younger audience but it's dark enough to please anyone. It still feels like horror fantasy but it behaves much more like a sadistic cartoon. The previous protagonists aged a bit and their paths all happen to converge to a specific block in New York City.

Most of the plot takes place in a prestigious high-tech high rise used for business, commerce and science, giving Gremlins 2 a prestigious stature. None of it is taken seriously and it's hilarious. When things go bad; worse than they've been so far, the makers' ambition and skills shine through. The creatures are now fully lit, revealing more and even better animatronics than 1984's Gremlins'.

The concept of metamorphosis is pushed further and turned into an ongoing joke. The actors are given intricate roles and are a colorful delight. The animation techniques used have evolved. The production quality is higher, too, and the sets are very atmospheric. Perfect gateway to horror for kids, Gremlins 2 chooses to be fun, surrealist and comedic but doesn't forget its more sinister roots.

THE SHINING
1980

8/8
Secluded in a remote hotel for the winter, a family is terrorized by ghosts.

The Shining is the ultimate ghost movie. It is not only about the dead coming back, but about vice, mental illness and human evil. It is a slow burn that never gets boring because when nothing happens, photography does. It is among Kubrick's best work and one of the best horror movies ever made. The hotel is a dense psychedelic labyrinth, and the script follows the same theme and logic.

Fans of thrillers get a thick depiction of family violence caused by alcoholism and supernatural lovers get scary ghosts. When mental illness and seclusion are gradually added to the equation, claustrophobia takes a new meaning. This is a long feature that constantly foreshadows, setting a stressful and uncomfortable tone that is as efficient psychologically as it is viscerally.

The set design is right out of a nightmare. The actors are so vigorous and meticulous it is troubling. Family horror, when approached so brilliantly, becomes something we can all relate to. It is never explicit about taboos, but quickly hints at many twisted concepts that make the movie highly rewatchable. Get ready to be immersed and shook up. Prepare for the horror experience of a life time!

Made in the USA
Middletown, DE
02 July 2022

68315482R00038